21st CENTURY FOSS

A Dragon's Dream Book

Editorial & Design:
11 Beaconsfield Villas
Brighton
Sussex BN1 6HA
England

Great Britain
Distributed by
Phin
Sunshine Industrial Estate
Churchill Road
Cheltenham, Gloucestershire
England

First Edition 1978

LIMPBACK: 0906196094

Text set in London
by APEX PHOTOSETTING

Printed in Holland
by CHEVALIER-ROTTERDAM

Colour separations
by CHEVALIER-ROTTERDAM

We would like to thank the following organizations for their co-operation with Dragon's Dream in the preparation of this book:
Aldus Books; Arrow; Corgi; Coronet; Fontana; Futura; Granada Publishing; Hodder & Stoughton; Hutchinson; Imagine Magazine; Island Records; J'ai Lu; Mayflower; Pan Books; Panther; Sphere; Star Books; The Sunday Times Magazine.

We would also like to thank these film companies for their permission to reproduce designs and drawings from the following projects:
Camera One: *DUNE;* Film Trust SA Panama: *SUPERMAN;* 20th Century Fox: *ALIEN.*

Very special thanks to the Hon. Michael Pearson, without whose generous help this book would not have been possible, to Alejandro Jodorowsky, and to Angus Wells, whose 'Profile of Chris Foss' was the basis for the introduction of this book.

CONTENTS

INTRODUCTION

Chris Foss shows us spaceships too big for planetary horizons to hold. The spectacle of his leviathans, glittering with lights and banded with the warning colours of poisonous insects or reptiles, confounds all expectation of scale. This achievement has placed him in the front rank of science fiction artists; his space hardware was the first to convey extra-terrestrial dimension convincingly. His paintings give form to intergalactic arks, ram-jetting or ion-driving entire civilizations from one remote star system to another. The only space in which these structures look at home is: Space.

Foss' imagery has captured the imagination to such an extent that he now commands a small army of imitators, movie designers included; think of the gargantuan starships and fabricated pseudoplanets of *Star Wars,* for example, and then look at the pictures in this book. It is no surprise that Foss now works directly on movie design and conceptualization, with film companies competing for his time.

But why do Foss' future conveyances and landscapes look so convincing? Foss suggests, with amusement, that his craft are "old fashioned and historic." This is true: his inventions evoke memories of Great War 'landships' and battleships, Edwardian liners, even Victorian suspension bridges. He says that they are "very tatty spaceships;" again, it's true that the explosions his craft endure in space-battle often leaves them scarred and blasted, limping home to monstrous, continental dry docks. But the curiously antiquated aspect of his work, as well as his meticulous eye for detail and scale, is why Foss' cities, ships, and transport systems occupy a reality of their own. They are simultaneously the precursors and the relics of the coming space age. Weary but functioning, they represent the everyday reality of a future accustomed to the extraordinary.

Chris Foss' past may help to explain his unique retrospective vision of the 21st century. He was born in 1946 in Devon, England. As a child he was fascinated by the remains of the Industrial Revolution, and explored the ageing railway tracks and disused mines that are still in evidence throughout the West Country. This interest led him to build models of railway lines and steam engines which he soldered up from whatever scraps of metal he could find. An art teacher encouraged his early ability with a pencil, and Foss took to sketching the surrounding countryside in between building his intricate railway models. The same teacher persuaded him to attempt a scholarship course that won him a place at a public school in Dorset.

Foss escaped the confines of that school as frequently as he could to sketch the semi-derelict shipyards and harbour installations at nearby Poole. At the same time he developed an interest in cars; he rebuilt and repainted car wrecks to create new workable machines. He was even then obsessed by speed, colour and hybrid technology. He also drew incessantly, recording his creations as they grew. Source material for his architectural imagination was provided by the huge fortifications constructed by the Nazis during their occupation of Guernsey. Foss often visited the island since he had family connections there. The fierce sunlight and harsh shadows in his work, the massive towers and ramparts punctuated by gun emplacements and look-out posts featured in his ships and cities may well be connected with memories of this fortress-island.

Influences, though, are only half the story; technique and reputation took much longer to establish. Foss' earliest ambition was to be an artist, but his family disapproved; so in 1964 he compromised and went to Cambridge University to study architecture. He soon discovered the grey limitations of the subject: "Architects have no conception of colour or of the presence that a building should impose." While at Cambridge he sold one-off cartoons to 'Autocar' and a six page cartoon strip to Bob Guccione's 'Penthouse' magazine. The contacts he gained through these efforts were to prove invaluable later, but when he dropped out of his course in 1966, he took a job with an architectural sculptor. It was not what he wanted to do, but it gave him a living and left him time to continue with his drawing and painting. He produced working drawings for mould assemblies and drew plans for sculpted features of new buildings, including the bronzed fibreglass rear facings for the doors of Liverpool Cathedral. He still sold artwork where he could, gradually developing his technique and style. In 1968 he bought an airbrush, "the only way I could see to get smooth gradations of pigment quickly," and at about the same time he found another lasting influence: his wife, Pat. He is now a happily married man with a daughter called Imogene.

The years from 1968 to 1970 were difficult for Foss. He left the architectural sculptor's office, and maintained himself and his wife by driving hire-cars in between long periods of drawing. Bob Guccione helped Foss greatly by putting him on a small retainer to produce theme drawings for an upmarket book in the 'Barbarella' genre: "I owe Bob a lot. My artwork wasn't up to commercial standards then, but he kept me going while I got there." And after the summer of 1969, which he spent driving cabs in Guernsey, all of these efforts paid off. A cover design for Constable Ltd., a publishing company, led to an introduction to a hard-selling design agency, and Foss' career entered a steady upswing. At first he tackled all kinds of book covers, "miscellaneous stuff, including some horrible disasters with figure work," but he gradually became sought after for his airbrushed scenes of warfare: planes, ships, submarines or starships. It was the starships, though, that really made his reputation.

The distinction of his futuristic work was obvious, yet unexpected. Hard and functional self-driving cities were juxtaposed with cloud-banked or galactic vistas. His structures were asymmetrical, immense, and totally unlike the needle-nosed and streamlined shapes favoured by his predecessors. Another influential innovation in Foss' work was colour: blacks, reds, blues and yellows converted his spaceships into interstellar waspships with a laser sting.

In the space of six years Chris Foss has become an international success. Authors like Isaac Asimov specifically ask for his work to illustrate their books. (One of his current projects is an illustrated version of Asimov's 'Foundation' trilogy.) His prolific output has brought him money, which he greatly enjoys and considers "as necessary as air for anybody, but especially a creative person." Books like 'The Joy of Sex' and 'More Joy of Sex', which he illustrated with delicate line drawings, testify to his artistic versatility. But at the moment the film industry is where his interests lie. He now finds himself in the fortunate position of being in demand for cinema work in the same way that he was sought after by art editors for science fiction cover design.

Double-page spread illustration for the Sunday
Times Magazine for an article on ESP.

Foss' first break into movies came in 1975 when Alejandro Jodorowsky, a brilliant
Paris-based film director with a cult following, saw some of his cover work. He was
engaged in filming Frank Herbert's science fiction classic *Dune*, and needed an artist to
conceptualize the far-reaching panoply of the Padishah Empire, together with the ships
and habitations of its sand-born opponents. Foss was called over to Paris in the autumn
of 1975, and found himself in a new world. Movie design offered him both a challenge
and the freedom to extend his imagination to previously unexplored dimensions.
Alejandro Jodorowsky's preface to the *Dune* section of this book suggests the atmosphere
into which Foss plunged himself, and gives an extraordinary personal account of Foss,
his work on *Dune,* and on science fiction projections in general. Unfortunately, the film of
Dune was never completed. It will be one day; and when it is, will most likely be designed
by Chris Foss.

The Coming of the Space Age. "This is the one that started it all. Commissioned by David Larkin, it was one of the first representational covers."

After the backers withdrew and the project folded, Foss came back to England and continued working on covers. But by now the cinematic grapevine had done its work and more film offers were to follow in quick succession. His first assignment was to conceptualize the planet Krypton for a movie based on *Superman*. Most recently, 20th Century Fox contacted Foss to see if he would work on concepts for *Alien*. He went to Los Angeles in June 1977, and worked for four months on the project. Since returning to England, he has taken on the conceptualization and design of three further films. On one he will be building the sets and will have control over all details of the visuals, including costumes.

Look at the drawings in this book. When these movies appear, there will be no question that Chris Foss is one of the finest science fiction artists working; at least, on *this* planet.

Left: Oil rig painting for advertising.

Right: Early pen sketch of German fortification in Guernsey.

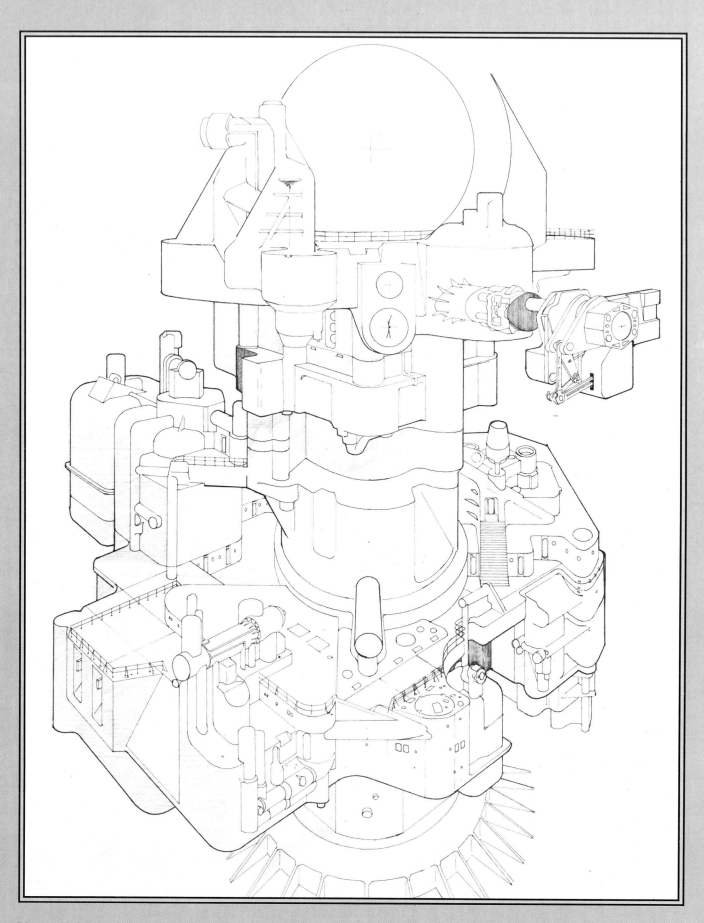

Line-work for drawing on page 13.

Birth Machine, early book project.

Dune had to be made.

But what kind of spaceships to use? Certainly not the degenerate and cold offspring of present day American automobiles and submarines, the very antithesis of art, usually seen in science fiction films, including *2001*. No! I wanted magical entities, vibrating vehicles, like fish that swim and have their being in the mythological deeps of the surrounding ocean. The 'galactic' ships of North American technocracy are a mouse-gray insult to the divine, therefore delirious, chaos of the universe. I wanted jewels, machine-animals, soul-mechanisms. Sublime as snow crystals, myriad-faceted fly eyes, butterfly pinions. Not giant refrigerators, transistorised and riveted hulks; bloated with imperialism, pillage, arrogance and eunuchoid science.

I affirm that next to the soul the most beautiful object in the galaxy is a spaceship! We all dreamed of womb-ships, antechambers for rebirth into other dimensions; we dreamed of whore-ships driven by the semen of our passionate ejaculations. The invincible and castrating rocket carrying our vengeance to the icy heart of a treacherous sun; humming-bird ornithopters which fly us to sip the ancient nectar of the dwarf stars giving us the juice of eternity. Yes! But far more than that: angelic splendour! We dreamed of caterpillar-tracked hotrods so vast that their tails would disappear behind the horizon. We saw ourselves enmeshed in these huge masses hurtling a dizzy train of planets from a dark world bound for a galaxy drowned in starry milk. We saw ourselves inside minute ether-dwelling sharks crossing seven thousand universes in one Terrene second, leaving a sound-wake freezing into a trail of hallucinatory pearls. Trains to carry away the whole of humanity; machines greater than suns wandering crazed and rusted, whimpering like dogs seeking a master. And great wings sucking the marrow of comets. And thinking wheels hidden behind meteorites, waiting, camouflaged as metallic rocks, for a drop of life to pass through those lost galactic fringes to slake thirsty tanks with psychic secretions. All this and more I wanted for *Dune*.

Then, suddenly, in a bookshop in the pages of an English magazine I found splashed in a thousand colours what I had believed impossible to depict. These spaceships that pleased and moved me were Chris Foss'. I covered the studio walls where I was preparing the film with his works. All masterpieces. I hired various sleuths to track him down. You see, in those heady days I had power! I had a multi-million dollar commitment behind me:

a commitment that remained unfulfilled. I had it in my power to call upon the best brains of our generation to collaborate on a project that was to give a messiah to the world. Not a human being, but a film. A film that would be our master. *Dune* had made me its apostle; but I needed others, and one of these was Chris Foss.

What the hell would this mutant be like? Because he had to be a mutant to draw like that! These were not drawings. They were visions! Would he be some neurotic old man? A maniac drug addict? Would one be able to talk to him? Then Chris Foss turned up, completely English with his tap-dancer's shoes, his tight suit as worn by Casanovas in sophisticated dives, with a tooth of quick-gold (I thought it was a diamond), with a yellow shirt of imperial silk, the blinding tie of an aesthetic hit-man, with a child's smile so penetrating he could turn into a hyena. Yes: Chris Foss was a true angel, a being as real and as unreal as his spaceships. A mediaeval goldsmith of future eons; a being who carried his drawings with the same ultra-maternal care as the Kaitanese Kangarooboos carry the children born of their self-insemination.

Chris arrived very nervous and mistrustful. He was afraid that we would impose a style on him, that we would limit him. But when he realized that he had total freedom he fell into ecstasy. He bought himself a special glass drawing-board which made his paper transparent, so that the lines seemed to float in space. And he plunged into his work for hours, millennia. He would go for long walks in the small hours to a little plaza where lepidopterous creatures with human skin and prehistoric perfumes would entwine their pink tongues with long, transparent hairs around his British member. I also saw him slake his physicoemoto-intellectuometaphysical thirst with alcohols seeping like tears from eyes slashed open in the aggressive air of a hotel corridor.

And thus were born the mimetic spaceships, the leather and dagger-studded machines of the fascist Sardaukers; the pachydermatous geometry of Emperor Padishah's golden planet; the delicate butterfly plane and so many other incredible machines, which I am sure will one day populate interstellar space. Chris Foss knows that today's technical reality is tomorrow's falsehood. Chris also knows that today's pure art is tomorrow's reality. Man will conquer space mounted on Foss' spaceships, never in NASA's concentration camps of the spirit. I was grateful for the existence of my friend. He brought the colours of the apocalypse to the sad machines of a future without imagination.

Jodorowsky

Alejandro Jodorowsky, 1977.

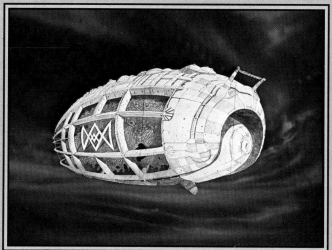

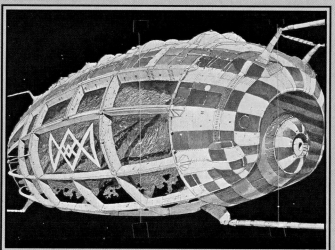

Top: Spice Container, design for *Dune*. 1975.

Bottom left: Sketch for Spice Container.

Bottom right: Spice Container.

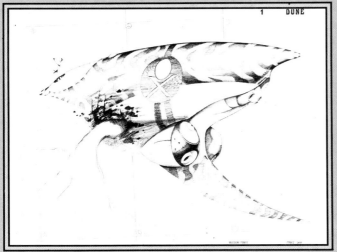

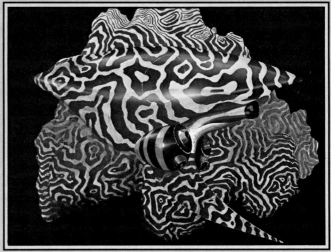

Top: Shot-up pirate ship spilling spice. *Dune.*

Bottom left: *Dune* illustration.

Bottom right: Striated meteorite with camouflaged pirate ship in foreground. *Dune.*

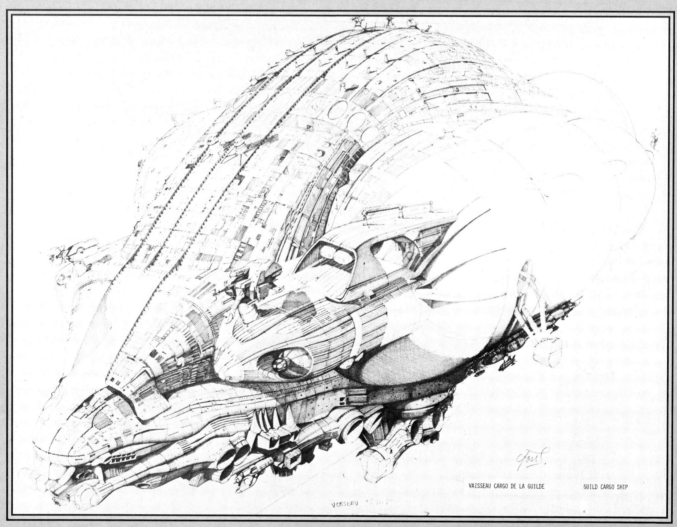

VAISSEAU CARGO DE LA GUILDE   GUILD CARGO SHIP

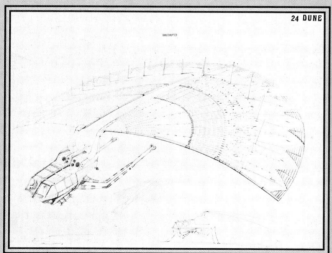

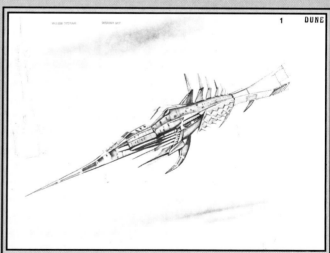

Top: Guild Merchant ship for *Dune*. Design requirement was for a large gross menacing ship.

Bottom left: Ornithopter, to be built as model. *Dune*.

Bottom right: Sardauker warship. *Dune*.

Top: The Emperor's Palace, in the centre of his
artificial planet. *Dune*.

Bottom left: Emperor's artificial planet.

Bottom right: Maquette design to be fabricated
in fibreglass: entrance ramp to Emperor's Palace.

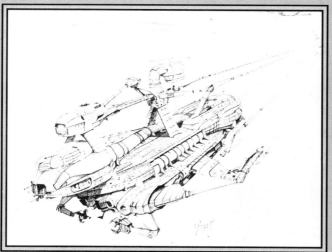 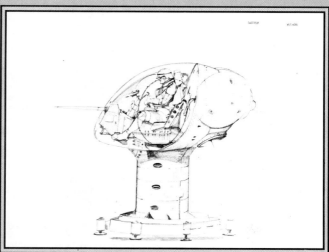

Top: Guild tug that pulls Spice Containers. *Dune*.

Bottom left: Earlier Guild tug design.

Bottom right: Early Sardauker warship.

LETOS CAR

Top: Leto's car. This would have been built on an adapted truck chassis, and was required to be capable of 60 m.p.h. It had to carry up to nine people, and mount a staircase. *Dune*.

Bottom left: Earlier version of Leto's car.

Bottom right: Top view, Leto's car. The gun turrets had to be occupied, and dead bodies would slide from the tailgate.

21

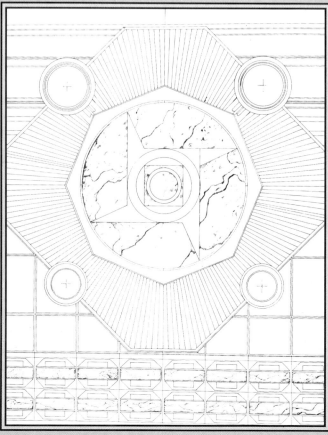

Left: The Emperor. Designed by Jean Giraud. *Dune.*

Right: Wall design for the Emperor's Chamber. The room revolved, and walls, floor and ceiling had repeating permutations of the same design.

Top left: Harkonnen flagship. *Dune.*

Top right: Harkonnen flagship.

Bottom left: Floating land machine, which would have been assembled in the Mexican Desert.

Bottom right: Energy-radiating column. One of a number which surrounded the Emperor's Palace.

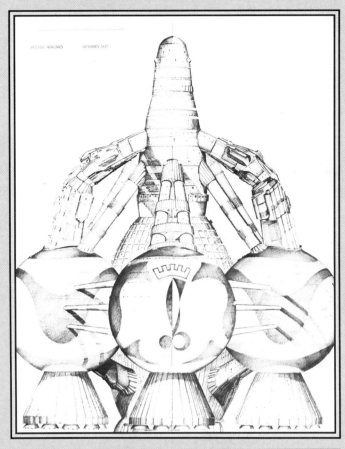

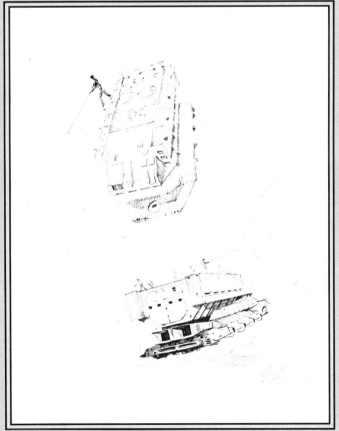

Top: General view, Krypton. *Superman*. 1976. The city was built on a crystal structure. At the start of the film the growths have begun to accelerate and the city is breaking up.

Bottom left: Derelict canal fractured by crystals. This picture appeared over the entrance of the Carlton Hotel at the Cannes Film Festival in 1976.

Bottom right: Hole in the wall, Krypton. Derelict buildings inhabited by outcasts.

Top: Main assembly buildings in Krypton. Abandoned structure in foreground.

Bottom left: Land machine take over by villain running amok.

Bottom right: View towards Superman's house, Krypton.

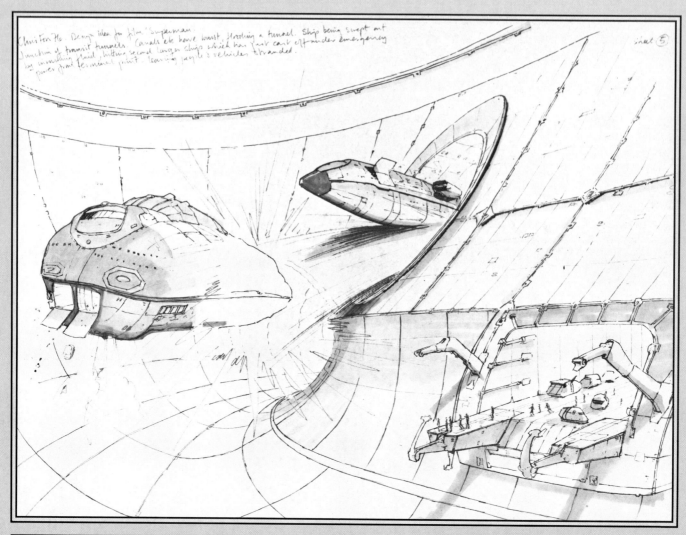

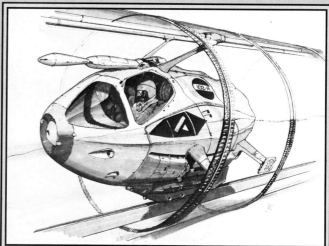

Top: Krypton breaking up. This view shows flooding in internal transit tunnel.

Bottom left: Ships negotiating crystal in transit tunnel.

Bottom right: Police vehicle in tube en route to Superman's house.

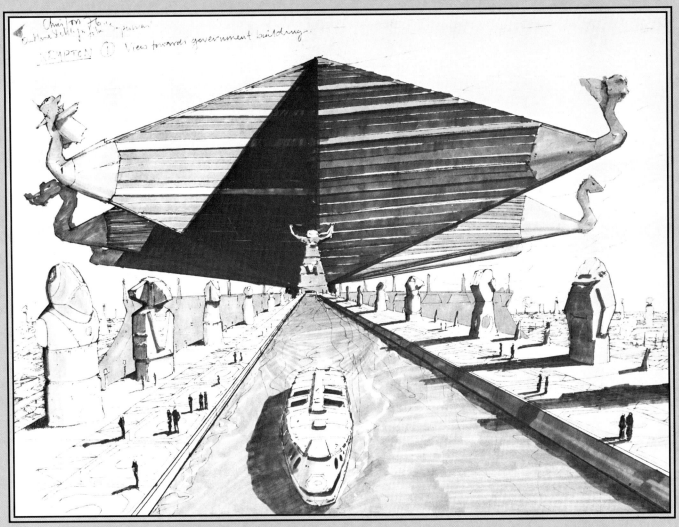

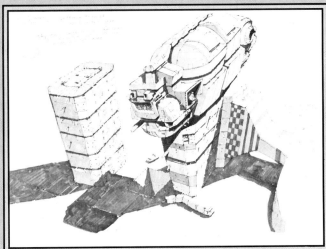

Top: Krypton before the disaster. View towards Palace building.

Bottom left: Another structure in Krypton city before the disaster.

Bottom right: Container-stacking vehicle. This was suggested location for villains to run amok.

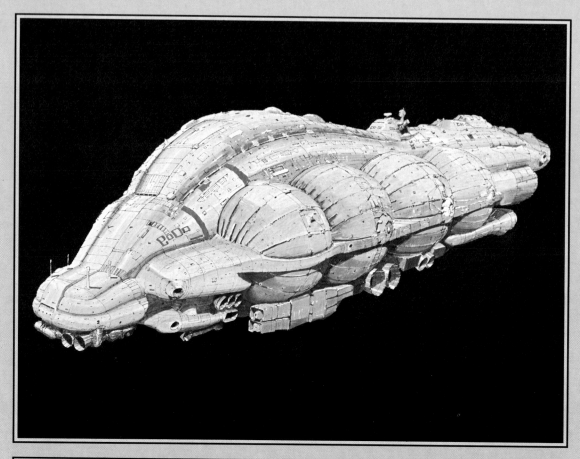

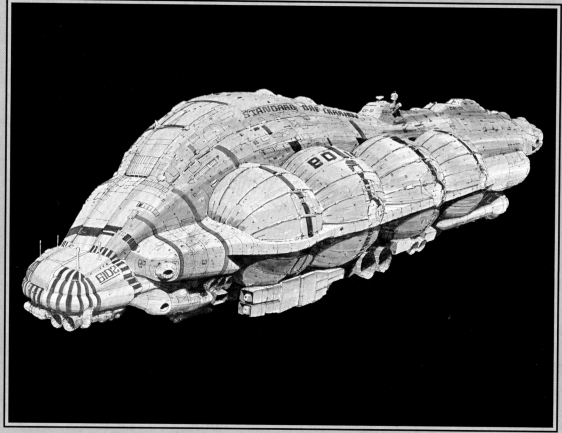

Top: Leviathan. All the action took place on this ship. *Alien*. 1977.

Bottom: Leviathan, different colour rendering. This is an adapted design of the *Dune* ship.

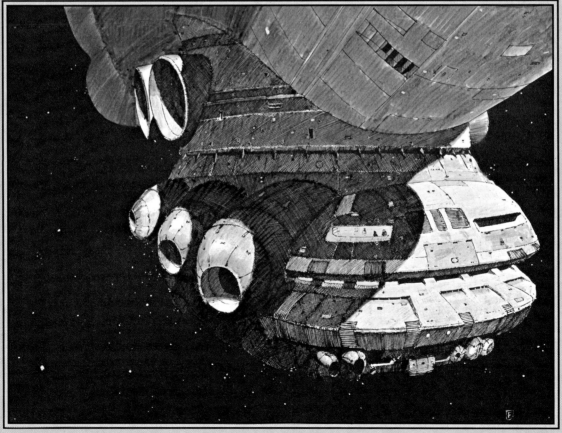

Top: A final survivor escaping from Leviathan.   Bottom: Alternative control-room design for Leviathan.

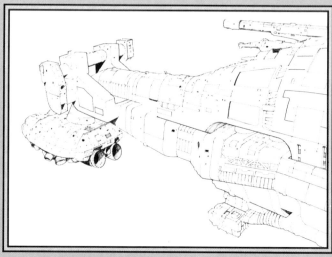

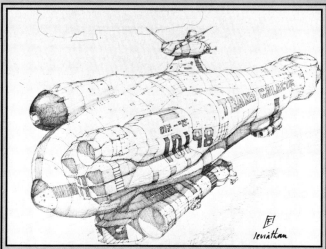

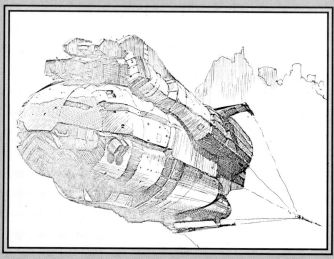

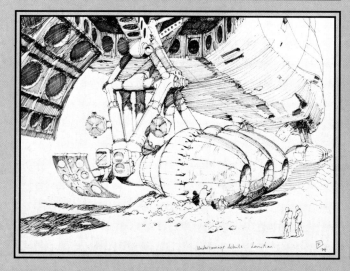

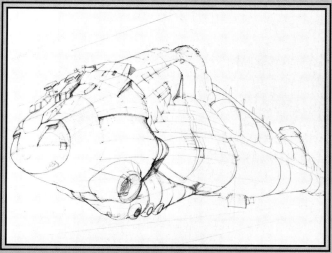

Top left: Alternative rear view for Leviathan.

Middle left: Leviathan.

Bottom left: Undercarriage of Leviathan, immediately after landing.

Top right: Front end, Leviathan.

Middle right: Smaller Leviathan, towing rock.

Bottom right: Line-work for Leviathan.

Top: Interior of the tomb with crew member descending shaft.

Bottom left: Oil refinery being pulled by Leviathan.

Bottom right: Alternative structure being towed by Leviathan.

20TH CENTURY WARFARE

The conning-towers of submarines and the superstructures of warships loom and roll through hostile waters, the fuselages of bomber planes overshadow nervous aircrews, and in the sky, fighters twist about each other as if inertia did not exist.

Foss' pictures of 20th Century Warfare are related to his visions of the future. They transmit the same conviction: this machinery is enormous or very very fast, and it works. There is a difference in scale and invention, of course. Foss can refer to memory and historical records for his images of submarines, tanks and aeroplanes. But he adds dynamism to this reference; he also gives his war machines life through their convincing scenarios: the empty deserts and blinding skies of North Africa; the ominous concrete and tarmac of East Anglian air fields; the high seas and storm clouds of the North Atlantic.

Look again at the landscapes and skies in Foss' paintings. They convey something of his admiration for Turner, the 19th century master of landscape, seascape and light.

El Alamein.

Top: *North Star Crusade.*
Bottom: *Hunter Killer.*

Top: *Scend of the Sea.*
Bottom: *The Watering Place of Good Peace.*

Top: *Action Atlantic*.
Bottom: Submarine with depth charge.

38

Top: *A Twist of Sand.*
Bottom: *The Bridge of Magpies.*

Submarine breaking surface.

One of Our Warships.

HMS Warspite.

Prince Eugen.

Top: One of a series of seven illustrations of   Bottom: same as above.
Freddy Forsyth's *The Shepherd*.

Top: Reader's Digest condensed book *Bomber*   Bottom: Tailpiece. Illustration for above.
by Len Deighton. Frontispiece.

Top: *Reach for the Sky* by Douglas Bader. Sketch.
Bottom: *Reach for the Sky*. Finished artwork.

Top: Airplane flying over Drem airfield. *Visitors from Outer Space*.

Bottom: *A Cleft of Stars*.

Top: *Bomb Run*.
Bottom: *A Grue of Ice*.

Top: Bombing of Nuremberg.

Bottom: Dogfight.

FUTURE PAST PROJECTIONS

Ion-driven Titanics, aluminium continents and miniature worlds roaming through the universe...Foss' vessels look as if the building of them took the resources of entire planets. Sometimes the starships swoop down onto convenient Terrene landing strips, guided by the perfect geometry of the pyramids perhaps, or drawn by the ready-made runways of Nazca.

Even when Foss' architecture is not derived from one specific ancient site it remains monolithic and imposing. Walls are always rampart, the bright bands of colour on Foss' structures always seem symbolic or ritualistic. The blending of these structures with the massive forms of his ships gives consistent scale to both. And of necessity, the robot-like machines that build, repair, or try to destroy these ships must be the size of mountains. It is strange that massive size should be conveyed through the precise drawing of tiny detail, but this is how Foss' inventions convey authenticity. Windows, flaps, hinges, and hatches are carefully worked out, then from these details the structure grows. Strong colours give the surfaces cohesion, and an even stronger presence.

The following section features starships, future cities, robots and artificial worlds. It ends with a thought for trans-atlantic pilots.

Landing Ground at Nazca.

The Secret Forces of the Pyramids.

The Great Pyramid.

Atlantis.

Away and Beyond.

Midsummer Century.

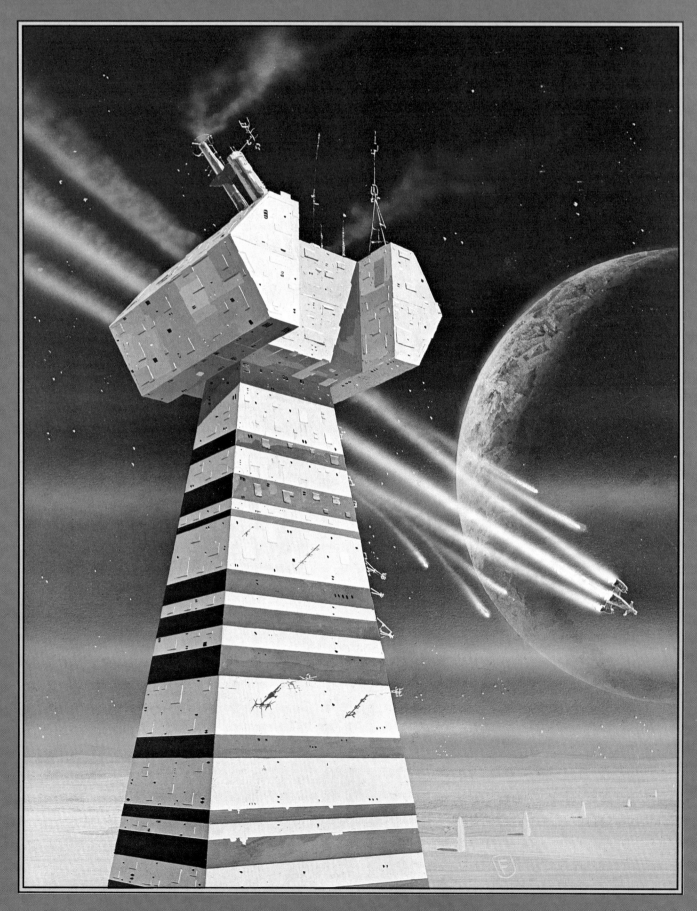

Invasion from Space.

Bomb being lowered into silo. *The View from the Stars.*

Torrent of Faces.

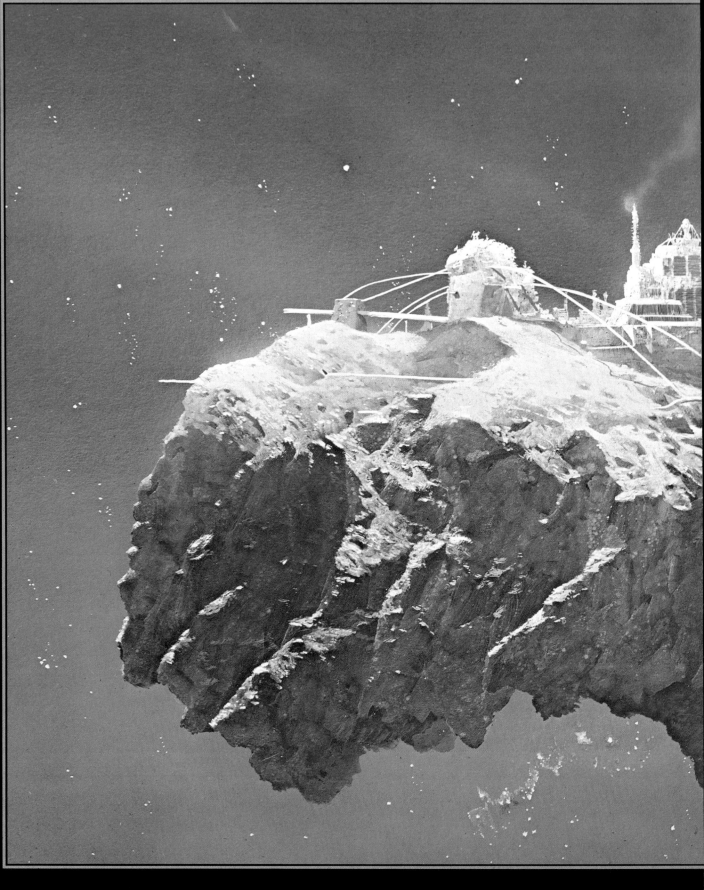

Cities in Flight.

Earth is Room Enough

Tomorrow's Children.

The Machine in Shaft 10.

Recalled to Life.

Large star-cruiser approaching floating city.
The Space Hounds of IPC.

Currents of Space by Isaac Asimov.

Asimov's *The Stars in their Courses.*

The Gods Themselves by Isaac Asimov.

SLAN.

Voyage of the Space Beagle.

Spaceship chasing meteorite.

Planets for Sale.

"The only cover I managed to paint in one day."
The Frederick Pohl Omnibus.

Aldus spaceship being pushed along laser beam.

The Patterns of Chaos.

Mission to the Stars.

Wanderers of Time.

Spacecraft lifting container.

Sub Space Explorers.

The Martian Way.

Galactic Corridors.

Galactic Riddle. Perry Rhodan.

The Ophiuchi Hotline.

Top: *The Rebels of Tuglan*. Perry Rhodan.   Bottom: *The Secrets of the Time Vault*. Perry Rhodan.

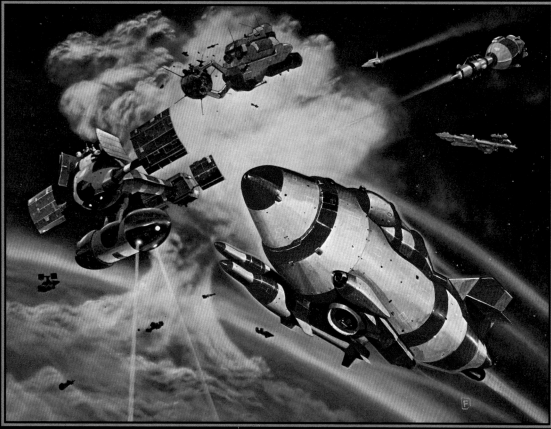

Top: *War in Space.*

Bottom: *Weapons of the Future.* CHIC Magazine double-page spread.

The Best of Arthur C. Clarke.

The Norman Conquest 2066.

The Radiant Dome. Perry Rhodan.

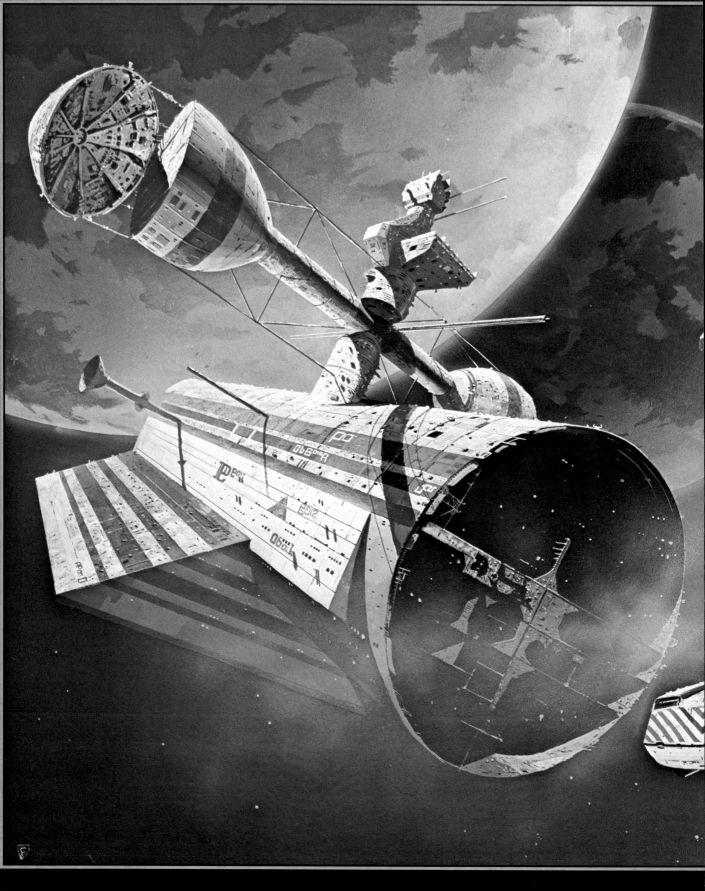

Spec painting for Futura Book.

Foundation Trilogy by Asimov.

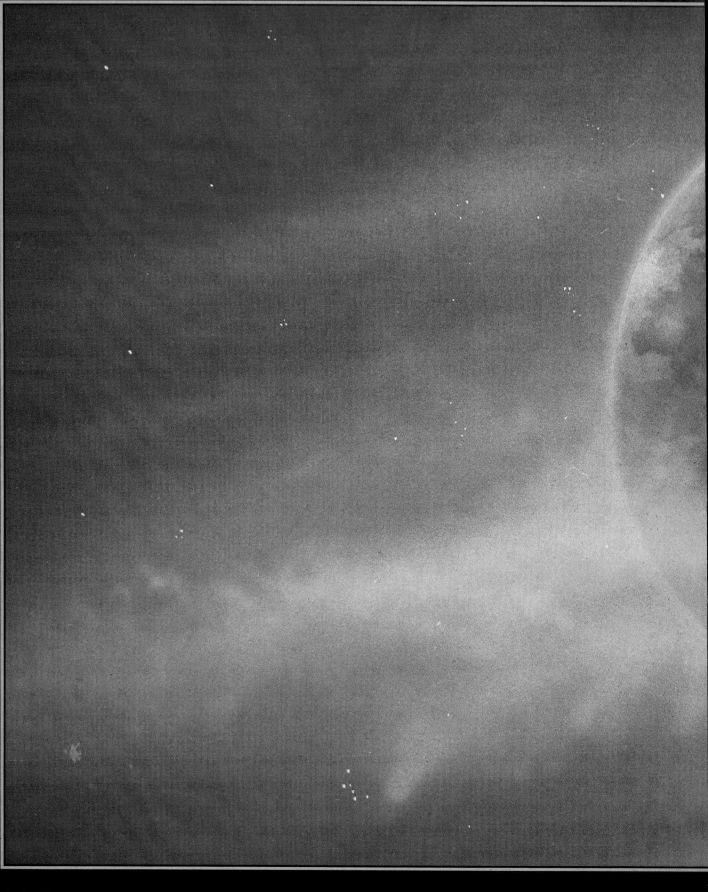

Jack of Eagles.

The Vega Sector. Perry Rhodan.

Top left and right: Chris Foss Book of Painting.

Bottom left: *Flesh*.

Bottom right: Chris Foss Book of Painting.

Chris Foss Book of Painting

Farewell Fantastic Venus.

The Galaxy Primes.

Bottom: *The Testament of Andros.*

Top: *A Case of Conscience.*
Bottom: *Quincux of Time.*

The New Improved Sun.

Quest in Time and Space.

Sea-Horse in the Sky.

Ian Gillan Band *Clear Air Turbulence* record cover.

Top: *Easter Island.*
Bottom: *Anywhen.*

Top: *Transit.*

Bottom: Edmund Cooper SF cover.

125

Top left: *A Frontier of Going.*

Bottom left: *Meltdown.*

Top right: *Stanley Spencer Spaceship.*

Bottom right: *Doc Smith.*

126

Top left: *Caves of Steel*.

Bottom right: Perry Rhodan 13.

Bottom left: *The Space Machine*.

127

Mutans vs. Mutans.

Mindbridge.

The Ufonaughts.

Top left: Spaceship in aerial dry dock.

Bottom left: *Catchworld.*

Bottom right: *The Earth Tripper.*

Top left: *Colony Earth*.

Top right: *The Stars in their Courses*.

Bottom left: *Someone Else is on Our Moon*.

Bottom right: *A Frontier of Going*. First Draft.

Top left: *LYDD* (became *Astounding Analog Reader*). Top right: Ground train passing abandoned working.
Bottom left: Robot Gun. Bottom right: *Earth's Last Fortress*.

Top: *Cauldron of Hell.*
Bottom: *All Fool's Day.*

Top left: *The Tungus Event.*

Bottom left: UFO.

Top right: *Is Anyone Out There?*

Bottom right: *Mayday!*

Crash by J. G. Ballard.

Kronk.

Top left: *The Cruise of the Conrad.*

Bottom left: *Raise the Titanic!*

Top right: *The Dove.*

Bottom right: *Drought.*

Top: *The Impossible Voyage.*
Bottom: *Historic Railway Disasters.*

Top: *The Stratocruiser Sighting.*
Bottom: *Tango November.*

Top: Mustang Airplane Chasing Flying Saucers.
(Visitors from Outer Space).

Bottom: Clouds.

LIST OF ILLUSTRATIONS